I Love You...

Bookmark Your Way
to a Remarkable Marriage

by Kelly Sopp

RUNNING PRESS
PHILADELPHIA

Running Press
Hachette Book Group
1290 Avenue of the Americas, New York, NY 10104
www.runningpress.com
@Running_Press

Printed in China

Published by Running Press, an imprint of Perseus Books, LLC, a subsidiary of
Hachette Book Group, Inc. The Running Press name and logo is a trademark
of the Hachette Book Group.

The Hachette Speakers Bureau provides a wide range of authors for speaking events.
To find out more, go to www.hachettespeakersbureau.com or call (866) 376-6591.

The publisher is not responsible for websites (or their content) that
are not owned by the publisher.

Print book cover and interior design by David Sopp

Library of Congress Control Number: 2020952064

ISBNs: 978-0-7624-7542-1 (hardcover), 978-0-7624-7543-8 (e-book)

1010

10 9 8 7 6 5 4 3 2 1

Contents

Happily.
Ever.
After.

That's the hope, right? To have a relationship that is untested, with hearts fully vested from the moment we say, "I do." We all want the romance we're promised in fairy tales, wedding magazines, and on the perma-grins of wedding-cake toppers. Each of us dreams of finding a partner who really understands us and challenges us to become our better selves. And despite a lot of us being the children of divorce, the devoted friends of divorcées, and perhaps even divorced once or twice ourselves, we still hold fast to the notion of everlasting love.

So can anyone hold the golden ticket to a golden anniversary? What exactly is it that makes some marriages not just survive, but thrive? After twenty-five years of getting it woefully wrong and wonderfully right in my own marriage, and listening to the stories of hearts around the globe, I can assure you that "Happily Ever After" is possible. It's even probable. As long as you're willing to do a little work.

This book is meant to help you communicate well, from your wedding day forward. I've tried to include everything that needs to be said in the course of a lifelong relationship, along with some practical wisdom for you to consider. I hope you find it so useful that the pages become yellowed and loose from years of heartfelt exchanges. Here's to marriage, and to making it remarkable!

How to Use This Book.

This book is a conversation. Pass it between you like a never-ending love letter. It's for all the things in your marriage that need to be said, or unsaid, or that simply aren't said often enough.

Don't worry. It's impossible to mess this up!

Under the front cover, you'll find a bookmark. Just mark a page, then leave the book in a surprising place for your partner to discover. Have fun with it! I've hidden it in my husband's sock drawer, leaned it against his coffee mug, and even buried it in a pile of laundry.

The sentiments are indexed and tabbed into categories to make it easy to find the words you're looking for. But in case you don't, I've included some blank pages to write your own.

Send a romantic message, deliver words of encouragement, work through a disagreement, apologize, or offer emotional support. You'll find anything is easier to say when it begins with *"Hey, I Love You . . ."*

How to respond? However you like! A laugh, a hug, or just being available to talk are all constructive ways to connect more deeply. Tuck the bookmark back in its pocket, or use it to deliver your heartfelt message in return. The words and actions you choose create the next page in your love story.

Love &
Marriage.

Love is usually described as some kind of accident. We fall into it. We are struck by it. Blindsided by it. Shot in the heart by the arrow of a mischievous cherub in the name of it. The great love stories usually contain an element of fate or destiny. A blind date. A chance encounter. Some statistical improbability of ever having even met. Love, if we're lucky, is a "thing" that happens to us. It's a feeling. It's a noun.

But what about marriage? How is marriage any different than love? I propose that marriage is a verb. It's an action. Something you do. It's to promise. Honor. Appreciate. Communicate. Understand. Encourage. Forgive. A truly great marriage isn't something that's a given. It's something that's made.

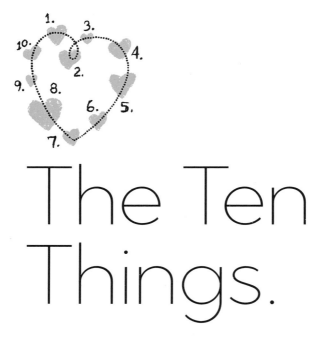

The Ten Things.

You know what would have been the most amazing wedding gift? A little white envelope. No, not even an envelope full of crisp hundreds! Just an envelope containing a handwritten list of ten things we could do to make our marriage remarkable. Admittedly, we probably would have tucked it away with all the other wedding cards, believing there would never come a day when we would need to work at being in love. But then one day, just as we'd be going adrift, we would rediscover the list of ten things and it would guide us home. Here's what I wish was on that list...

1. Never Stop Trying to Be the One.

Do you remember the moment you knew your spouse was the One? For some people, it's love at first sight. They just know. For others, it's a longer journey. My husband says that the first time he saw me, everything suddenly seemed different. He remembers the smallest of details about that moment. For me, though, love grew faithfully and slowly. He pursued me without smothering me, which I liked. When I was feeling overwhelmed or sad, he kept showing up for me. He made me laugh, he listened, and he made me feel beautiful.

 One afternoon, we were walking through North Beach in San Francisco. My stomach was tied up in knots because of a project at work. To my shock and embarrassment, I suddenly had to drop to my knees in the street and throw up. Now, most single guys would hightail it out of there at this point. But instead, he knelt beside me, held my hair back, and caressed my shoulders. That was the unglamorous moment that I knew he was the One! Through the ups and downs of life, he would be right by my side.

I know a gentleman who has been bringing home flowers to his wife every single day of his marriage. He began doing it when they were dating and he never stopped. But it isn't really about the flowers, is it? It's about the effort he puts into his marriage, every single day. Everyone loves to feel pursued. No matter how many years you've been in a relationship, if you keep trying to be the One, then chances are pretty good that you will keep being the One. Your spouse's affection is directly correlated to your effort. So why hold anything back?

2. Honor Each Other's Solitude.

Have you ever noticed while walking through the woods, that there's a natural distance between the trees? That's because all living things need space in order to thrive. If not, they overshadow one another trying to compete for the same light. In marriage, giving each other space allows each of you to find your light and grow stronger.

Over the years, I've come to believe that a certain amount of solitude is paramount to a healthy relationship. Because it's way too easy to become consumed by our partner's needs, or to smother them with our own! But when we are honoring each other's solitude, we are being mindful of each other's well-being. Naturally, we become more caring and giving. We learn to recognize when our partner isn't at their best, and respond with patience, protection, and the comfort of unwavering love. The urge to overshadow one another disappears.

 When my husband and I need space in our marriage, one of us will just say, "Can we have a choose-your-own-adventure night?" Then we're totally free to read, binge-watch TV, work on a project, play video games, or whatever, without the guilt of feeling like we're letting the other person down. Taking space can look like all kinds of things: travel; a fishing trip; tending a garden; sitting outside with an ice-cold beer to decompress; or just kicking your feet up on the couch at home. My husband's grandfather used to put on headphones and listen to music for hours. Whatever gives you space, give it value.

3. Always Speak Your Truth.

Why is it so darn hard to speak our truth? For many of us, it's because we're trying to please everyone around us. We know that speaking our truth could create

create conflict, so we suppress our own feelings for the sake of making things easier. But if you can be brave enough to speak your truth to the person you're sharing your life with, it will set you free from all kinds of needless agony.

Speaking your truth begins with taking the time to understand your own feelings, your purpose, and your passions. At first you might feel like this is selfish, but it's not. It only feels that way because we're taught to value the needs of others before our own. But isn't valuing yourself in the best interest of everyone? Doesn't caring for yourself allow you to better care for others? Just like the flight attendants tell you, put your own mask on first, then help those around you.

A few years ago, my husband and I were doing one of those silly *Cosmo* magazine personality quizzes. It revealed that we are both "Doormat Exploders"! Which means, we let people walk all over us until we've finally had enough and then we go ballistic. This was a revelation to us! We had never stopped to think about what people pleasers we are. But acknowledging this made it easier to spot our pattern of appeasing each other while pooling resentment. And over time, we've gotten a lot better at speaking our truths even when it makes us uncomfortable. We usually soften the conversation by starting with the words, *"Hey, I love you . . ."* because no matter what comes next, it's coming from a place of love.

4. Love Your Partner Selflessly.

From having sex to fixing a broken washing machine, there are about a gazillion ways we can express love in a marriage. The trouble is, it's not always in the way our partner is wired to recognize it. For example, one of the ways I like to express love for my husband is by cooking. I know it sounds like a 1950s homemaker cliché, but I really enjoy choosing recipes that I think he would like and shopping for the best ingredients to nourish him. But the truth is, he's just not that into eating! He enjoys being creative and productive, and he feels that stopping for breakfast or lunch (and sometimes even dinner) just slows him down. Instead, if I compliment his work or roll up my sleeves and help him complete a home project, he feels incredibly valued and loved.

Loving selflessly just means understanding how your partner feels most loved, and then loving them more in that way. It also means not attaching expectations to your gesture! If with every act of love we anticipate a reciprocal act of equal or greater measure, then our love isn't really a gift. It's a barter. And ultimately, it's a formula for disappointment. I've always found that love, when given selflessly, has a way of growing exponentially.

Would you believe we were married for two decades before we figured out that we recognize love differently? It's true! One evening, we were sitting by the fireplace and I asked him what the best part of his day was. He said, "When you helped me reglaze the windows." I laughed because that was literally the worst part of my day. But it prompted a great discussion about what makes us feel loved, and what expectations we had been placing on giving it. If you aren't sure what makes your partner feel most loved, just ask!

5. Give the Gift of Your Own Happiness.

Being happy is by far the greatest gift you can give to your spouse. One of the heaviest burdens in marriage is seeing the person you love struggle. It takes an incredible amount of energy to worry about whether your partner is happy, why they might not be, and how you can try to fix it. And the truth is, you can't. Happiness comes from within ourselves. When each of us takes on the responsibility of creating our own happiness, then we can show up for each other completely and our relationship can be filled with more joy.

This doesn't mean we shouldn't support each other! Sometimes loving means leaning. Especially when dealing with a crisis or a difficult trauma from our past. But you can be there emotionally for your partner, while also encouraging them to heal by seeking the additional help and resources they need.

Look, every day isn't going to be a good one. Some mornings, I find myself rushed and stressed out and embarrassingly short-tempered. By the time I finally get over it, I've already passed my bad mood on to my husband like a virus. The lesson here is, how we show up for our marriage each day matters. Negativity radiates. So does happiness.

6. Be a Really Good Apologizer.

The two most important words in a marriage are "I'm sorry." Because the fact is, no matter how completely incredible and amazing you are, there will be days when you hurt your partner's feelings, let them down, or make them want to pack a bag and head straight for the Florida Keys. For the first twenty-four years of my marriage, I was a terrible apologizer! I thought I was doing it right, but nope. I had it terribly wrong. My lips were saying words I thought sounded like an apology, but I was really just making excuses for my actions. Not at all the same. I can't tell you how many times I've had to reapologize for a crappy apology.

A true and proper apology is a way forward. No matter who's right and who's wrong, saying I'm sorry is an acknowledgment of the other person's feelings and a testament to love that is worth humbling ourselves for. Life is long, and it's inevitably going to be filled with arguments. But life is also too short to waste a minute being angry about something you probably won't remember this time next year.

What makes a true and proper apology? Saying the words "I'm Sorry" for something you did, without using the word "but," and offering reparation while asking for nothing in return. (Then, I advise you to zip your lips while you're ahead.)

7. Celebrate Each Other Often.

Celebrating each other is both an act of gratitude and an acknowledgment of personal growth. There's something so powerful about taking a moment to pause and reflect on your individual accomplishments and your joint achievements. And I'm not just talking about the big things! Little things like paying off a bill, or cleaning out your closet, deserve to be celebrated, too. It's a way of filling our lives with positivity.

 It can be raising a glass to toast the end of a long day, presenting a hand-sketched award, going out for a special dinner, or taking a big vacation. Whatever it is, let it bring you joy. Life has plenty of challenges, so it's important to high-five the wins.

Many of the kind and remarkable things we do as spouses go unnoticed. That's because we get used to these things over time and we start taking them for granted. My husband makes me a cup of coffee every morning, which is a gesture of thoughtfulness. But I've caught myself expecting the cup to be waiting for me and even forgetting to say thank you! But if I'm celebrating him, I sit down next to him on the couch for a few minutes, enjoy the coffee, and talk about our hopes and plans for the day.

8. Become Best Friends with Benefits.

When you can relax in the comfort of knowing your partner loves you for exactly who you are, then you are experiencing the very best kind of friendship. And when you can be intimate inside of that friendship, you are experiencing the deepest kind of love.

 I know, I know. Everyone jokes about how once you get married it's the end of your sex life. But it shouldn't be! A marriage counselor once told me that intimacy is what makes you more than roommates. Experiencing physical pleasure within the safety of a lifelong commitment means you have permission to explore what really makes each of you happy. And trust me, it's a lifelong learning process!

Newlywed sex is totally different than I'm-exhausted-from-work-I-just-want-my-sweatpants sex, which is totally different from vacation sex, which is totally different than makeup sex, which is totally different from let's-have-a-baby sex. And, yes, there are naturally going to be long stretches where life is just a lot and you can't be bothered. But marriage is a marathon, not a sprint. The key is to keep showing up. Naked.

9. Be Brave by Allowing Yourself to Be Vulnerable.

One of the hardest things to do, even with a person you love and trust, is to allow yourself to be vulnerable. It's natural to want to protect ourselves from the ways in which we've been hurt before. It's natural to want to put on a thick skin and say, "I'm fine." Most of us would much rather overcompensate in our areas of strength than reveal we have weaknesses. But you can't be honest without being vulnerable. And relationships that are rooted in honesty have a much better chance of working out.

I know a man who hid financial problems from his wife for years. He made a bad business deal, took out a second mortgage on their home to pay off debt, secretly borrowed money from friends and relatives, and just kept on pretending everything was fine. Only, it wasn't. Of course his wife eventually found out, and the dishonesty nearly split them up. If only he had allowed himself to be vulnerable and admit he was in over his head, they could have faced the situation together as a team.

I honestly believe there is nothing more brave than admitting what you're afraid to own up to. Worries, troubles, and fears, as well as hopes, desires, and dreams, can all be managed if they can be mentioned. So get vulnerable. If anyone has your back, it's the spouse at your side.

10. Remember How Lucky It Is to Be Loved.

When it's impossible to get a restaurant reservation on Valentine's Day, and TV shows like *Say Yes to the Dress* are heading into their nineteenth season, it's easy to assume that love comes easy. But ask your single friends to weigh in on the ease of finding a soul mate and they'll likely tell you a different story. In fact, let's do a little math.

The odds of you being born at all are less than one in four hundred trillion. Basically, you're a miracle. The odds of your spouse being born are also less than one in four hundred trillion. Again, a freakin' miracle. Of the six billion adults on the planet, only 70 percent report experiencing love on a daily basis. Around 58 percent are married. Which means, at this very moment, there are at least two billion people in this world who are still hoping to find someone special to split a pizza with.

What are the odds of you having found your spouse? Factoring in all the possible variables like, what if you were five minutes late and missed the bus that day? What if you had a cold and didn't go to that party? What if you decided not to log in to your dating app? I think you would agree the odds are infinitesimal.

My point is this: It's incredibly lucky to be loved. *You* are the one person, out of all the other amazing and eligible people in this world, that your partner chose to hold close for the rest of their one-in-four-hundred-trillion-odds of a life.

Fireworks Begin with a Spark.

What is romance? Sparks! Your words have the power to ignite your love for each other, each and every day. So I hope you wear this section out!

Bookmark something sweet. Or maybe suggestive. Show your admiration. Express your gratitude. Share what's in your heart. You don't have to be a poet to be a romantic, just be yourself! But if you do have a way with words, you can use the blank page to get creative.

You're
Beautiful.

Seriously, you

take my breath away.

Kiss Me.

What do I have to

do to get a smooch
around here?

How Did I Get So Lucky?

Being with you is
my biggest win.

Could We Cuddle?

Nothing would feel better than
just curling up next
to you.

Let's Make a Baby!

I couldn't be
more excited to build
a family with you.

Let's Play Hooky!

What do you say we blow off our responsibilities and go have some fun?

I Want
to Be on
Vacation
with You.

I want to eat vacation food, have vacation sex, and wear vacation clothes!

You're So Smart.

You've got the most amazing mind, and it just blows me away sometimes.

Could You Be Any More Handsome?

Answer: No.
You're A-list
movie-star level.

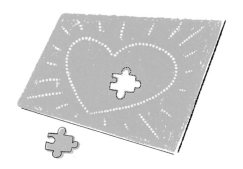

I Need You.

The life I want
only works with
you in it.

You're the
Best Thing
That Ever
Happened
to Me.

It's true.

I'm entirely grateful
for the day I met you.

I'm Better Because of You.

You make me
want to live up to
my potential and be
my best self.

You
Amaze
Me.

Just when
I think I know
everything about
you, there you
go impressing
me again.

I'm Glad You're on My Team.

It feels good
knowing that we've
always got each
other's back.

I Appreciate
You.

I might not
tell you this enough,
but I'm so grateful
for who you are
and all you do.

Ha Ha
Ha

You Always
Know How
to Make
Me Laugh.

Your sense of humor is one of my favorite things about you.

You're
a Good
Human.

I wish there were
more people like you.

You Look Great.

Have I told you how fantastic you look lately? Wow. Just wow.

I Want You.

I'm so attracted
to everything
about you.

You Totally Get Me.

It's so nice
that I can be myself
around you.

I Like
Hanging
Out
with You.

It doesn't matter
what we're doing,
it's just fun being
with you.

You're
My Best
Friend.

In fact, you're

my favorite person in
the whole world.

I Hit the
Jackpot.

I mean, what are the chances someone like me could marry someone like you?

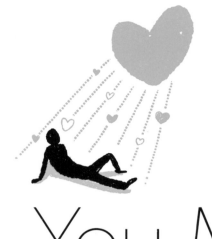

You Make Me Feel Good.

The way you see me is the way I wish I could always see myself.

You Light Up a Room.

You have a way
of brightening
everyone around you.
You're luminous.

Not Just
a Soulmate.
A Teammate.

Encouragement

Sometimes we believe in the person we love more than they believe in themselves. A few well-timed words of encouragement could foster the confidence they need to thrive. Even though it's tempting to want to fix things for our partner, all we really need to do is to show them we care. So be generous with your support for each other. I'm a big fan of stopping to celebrate the wins, no matter what size. It lets you both fully experience the joy of your commitment!

You've
Got This!

You were built
for this moment.
You're totally ready.

I'm So
Proud of
You.

Seriously,

I'm so proud. Look what you've done.

Keep
Going!

Just keep
showing up for
yourself. It will all
be worth it.

I'm So
Happy for
You!!!!

Yay! Hooray!

I can't even fully
express how thrilled
I am for you.

It Gets
Easier.

Trust me,
things won't be
difficult forever.
There are better
times ahead.

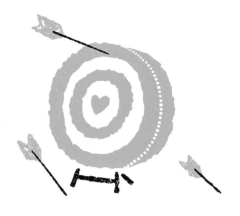

Give
Yourself
Grace.

It's okay,

you're learning!
Improvement comes
from making mistakes.

Please
Help Me.

I'm overwhelmed and I'm humbly asking for your assistance.

You're Crushing It!

It feels so
great to watch you
doing so well.

Am I Doing Okay?

I'm not even sure anymore. How do you think I'm doing?

What Do You Need?

It's okay to tell me. And please let me know if I can help.

You're
So Brave.

I really admire
your ability to face
hard things.

Trust Your Instincts.

What is your
gut telling you?
Your internal voice is
usually right, even if
it's a whisper.

I Believe in You.

I have 100% faith that you're completely capable of whatever you set your mind to.

Maybe You Need a Break.

Sometimes a
little distance can give
you renewed energy
and more clarity.

Please
Push Me.

I could really
use your help
staying motivated.

Good Things Are Coming Your Way.

You deserve it.
Have faith that
blessings are just
around the corner.

You're
Not Alone.

There are a lot
of people who love
and support you,
including myself.

You Are
Stronger
than
You Know.

It wouldn't
surprise me at all
if you sailed right
through this.

Nothing
is Wasted.

Everything
you are working at
right now will have
meaning and value.

Have Patience.

There's a right time for everything, and it will come.

We Did It!

I'm so proud of us.
Look what we
achieved together!

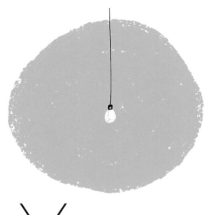

You
Matter.

You're important

to so many people.
Including me.

Things Are Looking Up!

Finally, there's a bright spot. Here's to better days ahead.

You're
Powerful.

The things

you say and do will
have lasting impact.

Let's Celebrate!

Cheers!

What do you say
we make time to
acknowledge this
great moment?

You Mean
Everything
to
Someone.

Whether one of you is going through tough stuff, or it's the both of you, the beauty and grace of a relationship is that you can face it together. Bringing up a subject that you've been afraid to talk about can lift the weight off your conscience. Or, it can be a lifeline that pulls your partner out of real trouble. I've discovered over the years that empathy encourages healing. A simple expression of solidarity can mean everything to someone who feels lost in the woods and the only way out is through.

I'm Worried About You.

It seems like you might be having a tough time right now. Want to talk about it?

We'll Get Through This.

Just know,
we're in this together.
And with you by my
side, I feel like we can
do anything.

It's Going
to Be Okay.

It may take some time. But eventually, everything will be as it should be.

I'm Really
Sorry about
What You're
Going
Through.

It must be tough.
I'm here for you
whenever you
need me.

Hold Me.

Hey, babe,
I could really use a
great big hug.

It's Not You. It's Me.

You haven't
done anything wrong,
I promise. I'm just
struggling today.

I'm
Exhausted.

I could face-plant into my pillow right now and sleep for days.

I Need
to Speak
My Truth.

It never seems like the right time to bring it up. So could we make time?

You're My Lighthouse.

You guide me through the dark times. Thank you.

I Think We Need Some Help.

I'm feeling like
it might be time for
us to get some
professional support.

Maybe There's a Lesson in This.

It might be hard
to see it now,
but time will give us
a better perspective.

I Will
Never
Give Up
on You.

Please know that

I am here for you.
Forever.

I Need Help.

I think this is more than I can handle on my own.

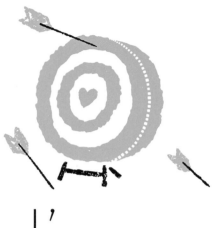

I'm
Trying.

Really, I am.
Please be patient
with me.

We've
Been
Through
Worse.

This is hard.
But we've survived
harder things before.

Is Something Wrong?

I just have this
feeling that
something's not right.

It's Just a Bump in the Road.

We're going to have setbacks once in a while. But we'll get past them.

I Can't Wait to Look Back on This and Laugh.

Someday we'll
be so far past this
that we'll be able to
have a sense of
humor about it.

Being in
Love Feels
Better
than Being
Right.

Marriage is a union of two individuals. And as individuals, we are absolutely allowed to have our own thoughts, opinions, and beliefs. People who love each other can also argue. Disagreements are not the end of the world, nor do they signal the end of a marriage. What's ultimately important is valuing the relationship above all else. This means keeping an open heart. And a small ego. It means respectfully communicating.

Let's Talk This Out.

The only way past this, is through this. Let's sit down together and figure this out.

Life's Too Short to Fight.

What do you say we call a truce and move on to bigger and better things?

You Hurt
My Feelings.

Ouch.

I could really use an apology. Or maybe an acknowledgment of how I feel.

Are You Mad at Me?

If you are,
could you please help
me understand why?

Thanks
for the
Apology.

I'm still processing my feelings, but thank you for telling me you're sorry.

I Forgive You.

I want you
to know that I'm
letting it go.

Are We Okay?

That was tough.

I just want to check that we're in a good place.

I Appreciate
Your
Honesty.

Thank you for
being real with me
and speaking
your truth.

I Want You to Understand.

Please allow me

to really explain.

You Make
a Good
Point.

I've been thinking about what you said and I can see where you're coming from.

Let's Compromise.

How about we meet in the middle? That way, we can both be happy.

I Have Some Questions.

May I ask them?

I'm still just a little
bit unclear.

Let's Kiss and Make Up.

Nothing would feel better than resolving this and getting back to normal.

Can I Get Something Off My Chest?

Could you listen
while I just vent?
There's something
that's been weighing
on me.

Please
Let It Go.

My heartfelt advice is to try and let go of what's troubling you.

Say It
Like You
Mean It.

Apologizing is undoubtedly one of the hardest things to do correctly. Offer up a bad apology and you'll discover that you have two things to apologize for! Here are some carefully written apologies to help you out. If you don't see one that suits your particular situation, use the rules of a good apology to construct your own.

Rules for a good apology:

1) Say the words "I'm Sorry" for something you did.

2) Do not use the word "but."

3) Offer reparation while asking for nothing in return.

I'm Sorry
I Hurt Your
Feelings.

I was being a real jerk. Please know that I'll be trying to redeem myself through small acts of kindness.

I'm Sorry
I Argued
with You.

I know we don't agree, and that's okay. I will try harder to understand your perspective.

I'm Sorry for Not Helping.

I haven't been pulling my weight lately. Please let me know how I can help you out.

I'm Sorry for Overreacting.

I've had time to think, and honestly, it's just not worth being that upset about. I'd love to move past this.

I'm Sorry
I Didn't Do
What I Said
I'd Do.

You should be able
to count on me.
Next time, I'll make
sure I keep my word,
and follow through.

I'm Sorry
for Letting
My Anger
Build Up.

I will try to be a better communicator when something is bothering me from now on.

I'm Sorry
for Making
You Worry.

I know it caused you grief. In the future, I'll make sure to let you know how I'm doing.

I'm Sorry
I Wasn't
There
for You.

I failed to show up when you needed me. Next time, I will do better.

I'm Sorry
for What
I Did.

I regret it terribly.
And while I can't undo it,
I can promise that I will
never do it again.

I'm Sorry
for Not
Listening
to You.

I was wrong and
I fully admit it. I will learn
from this experience.

(Not) The
End of
the Book.

Surprise! This book doesn't have an end. What you're holding is a beginning and a middle. That's because each day that we get to wake up next to the person we love is a chance to create the narrative of our love story. It's a chance to grow closer, to love more deeply, to listen better, to understand each other more. In a love story, we need ever only find ourselves in the middle. Tomorrow we can mark a different page.

Index

Tough Times

Disagreements

Apologies

Bibliography

Binazir, Ali. "Are You a Miracle? On the Probability of Your Being Born." *The HuffPost*, June 16, 2011.
https://www.huffpost.com/entry/probability-being-born_b_877853.

Friedman, Uri. "Map of the Countries that Feel the Most Love in the World." *The Atlantic*, February 14, 2014.
https://www.theatlantic.com/international/archive/2014/02/map-the-countries-that-feel-the-most-love-in-the-world/283839/
http://cf.datawrapper.de/x1foC/4/.

Institut national d'études démographiques (INED). "Are There More Men or Women in the World?" Updated May 6, 2020.
https://www.ined.fr/en/everything_about_population/demograpic-facts-sheets/faq/more-men-or-women-in-the-world/.

Ortiz-Ospina, Esteban, and Max Roser. "Marriages and Divorces." 2020.
https://ourworldindata.org/marriages-and-divorces.

Robbins, Mel. "How to Stop Screwing Yourself Over." Filmed June 2011 in San Francisco, California. TED video, 21:39.
https://www.ted.com/talks/mel_robbins_how_to_stop_screwing_yourself_over?language=en.

Acknowledgments

It takes so much more to write a book than writing the book. What I mean is, I wholeheartedly believe were it not for the following people, this book would not exist in the way that it does. Thank you to my husband, David, for the love and collaboration you've put into our relationship over the past twenty-five years. I will cherish all the years I am lucky enough to be on this planet with you. To my son, Atticus, your encouragement has meant the world to me and I always hope to make you proud. Thank you to my talented editor, Jennifer Kasius, for your thoughtful feedback, which led to a better book to put into this world. I'm deeply grateful to Phyllis Klaus and Betty Hutcheson, two incredible therapists who've helped me navigate life's challenges and become a better partner. To my parents, Ron and Linda, thank you for setting an exceptional example of commitment. And to my friends and family, at home and abroad, thank you for demonstrating what the human heart is capable of.

About the Author and the Illustrator

Kelly met David in San Francisco in 1991, and they've been creating their version of a love story ever since. She's a writer who overthinks most situations, is woefully unorganized, loves cooking without a recipe, collects audio soundbites, prefers non-fiction, can't watch scary movies, and feels at home around trees. David is an illustrator & designer who laughs at most situations, always has a checklist, loves a wide range of music, collects vintage objects, prefers history books, has really seen a ghost, and feels totally out of place on a beach. They have a son, Atticus, who they both agree is their greatest blessing. Kelly and David share a philosophy that nobody in this world really knows what they're doing, but together, you can figure it out. Currently, they live in North Carolina.

Find extra bookmarks
and other inspiration
at heyiloveyoubook.com.